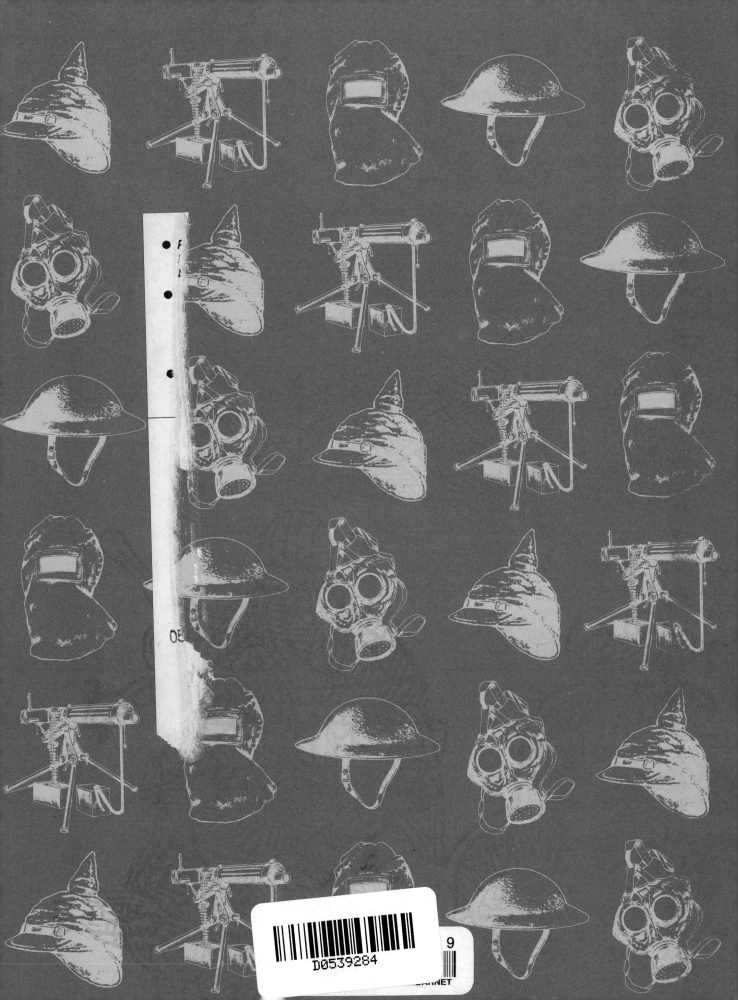

ARMIES OF THE PAST

GOING TO WAR IN
WORLD
WAR ONE

ARMIES OF THE PAST

GOING TO WAR IN
WORLD
WAR ONE

Adrian Gilbert

FRANKLIN WATTS
LONDON•SYDNEY

ILLUSTRATIONS BY

Mark Bergin
Kevin Maddison
Lee Montgomery
Steve Noon
Peter Visscher
Maps by Stefan Chabluk

Editor Penny Clarke
Editor-in-Chief John C. Miles

Designer Steve Prosser
Art Director Jonathan Hair
Picture Research Susan Mennell

© 2001 Franklin Watts

First published in 2001
by Franklin Watts
96 Leonard Street
London
EC2A 4XD

Franklin Watts Australia
56 O'Riordan Street
Alexandria
NSW 2015

ISBN 0 7496 4042 1

Dewey classification: 940.3

A CIP catalogue record
for this book is available
from the British Library.

Printed in Hong Kong, China

CONTENTS

The road to war

In 1914 Europe was divided into two hostile groups of countries. Germany and Austria-Hungary were called the Central Powers. They were opposed by the Allies: Russia, France, Britain and Belgium.

The leaders of the Central Powers believed that war would break out eventually, and that it would be better for them if it happened quickly. They began to look for an excuse to go to war, and they found it when Austrian Archduke Franz Ferdinand was shot dead by Serb nationalists in Sarajevo.

When Austria-Hungary demanded Serbia's virtual surrender, Russia said it would come to Serbia's aid. The rest of Russia's allies followed, and a large-scale conflict became inevitable.

The assassination of Archduke Franz Ferdinand
Relations between Serbia and Austria-Hungary were already bad, and this incident led to the outbreak of war.

PORTUGAL

Canada
Britain
Pacific Ocean
USA
Russia
Atlantic Ocean
Japan
ATLANTIC OCEAN
WORLD MAP 1917
Togoland
AFRICA
Dutch East Indies
India
New Guinea
Cameroon
German East Africa
New Zealand
Allied Powers
German South-west Africa
Australia
Central Powers

WORLD WAR ONE YEAR BY YEAR

The war begins, 1914
The Central Powers declare war against Russia and France. Germany marches through Belgium to attack France, and Britain joins the Allies.

The war develops, 1915
A trench system extends across western Europe. Germany uses poison gas against the Allies. The Russians are pushed back by a major German offensive (attack). Allied landings at Gallipoli against the Turks fail.

Western Front, 1916
A German offensive against the French at Verdun is stopped at great cost. An Allied offensive along the River Somme also causes heavy casualties but doesn't produce a victory for either side.

The Treaty of Versailles
Signed in 1919, the Treaty of Versailles brought the war to a formal close.

The Central Powers of Germany and Austria-Hungary were forced to admit defeat; Germany lost territory, while the Austro-Hungarian Empire was disbanded.

Germany also had to pay reparations (money) to the Allies.

MAP OF EUROPE 1914

MEDITERRANEAN SEA

■ **Allied Powers**	□ **Central Powers**	┈┈ **Western front line of trenches 1914**
■ **Countries joining Allied Powers**	■ **Countries joining Central Powers**	■ **Neutral Countries**

⚔ **Major battle sites**

⛵ **Sea battle of Jutland**

The naval war, 1916-17
British and German fleets fight at Jutland. Neither side wins outright, and the Germans are unable to break the British naval blockade of their ports. The Germans use submarines to attack British shipping.

Year of decision, 1917
The United States enters the war on the Allied side. Once American armies are trained and ready, Germany is outnumbered. The Russian army begins to collapse as revolution topples the Tsar.

Defeat of Central Powers, 1918
American troops and equipment help the Allies defeat the Germans on the Western Front. The Germans ask for peace talks in November, by which time Austria-Hungary and Turkey have already collapsed.

Off to the front

Once war had been declared, the young men of each nation were called up, or mobilised, by the army.

In most nations, when males reached the age of 17 or 18 they had to serve for up to two years in the army. The idea behind this was that if war broke out, each nation could call upon men who had been given some military training. These men were called conscripts.

Germany, for example, had a peacetime army of 870,000 regular soldiers, but in 1914 it could mobilise a total of 4.3 million men.

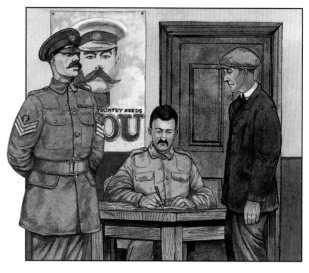

RECRUITING CIVILIANS

Many men who were not conscripts volunteered to fight for their country. Britain relied heavily on volunteers. In 1914 hundreds of thousands of men were recruited into the army.

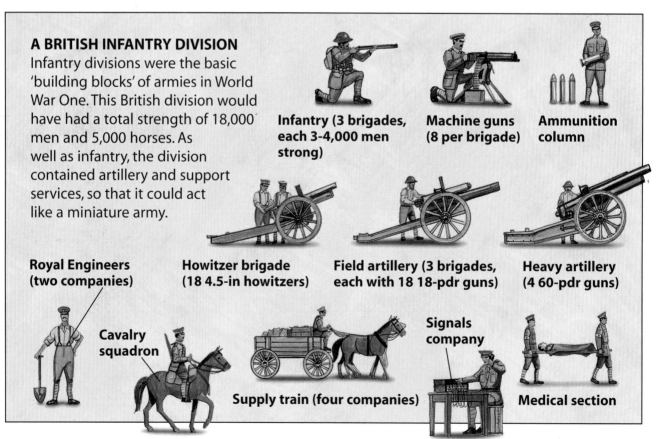

A BRITISH INFANTRY DIVISION

Infantry divisions were the basic 'building blocks' of armies in World War One. This British division would have had a total strength of 18,000 men and 5,000 horses. As well as infantry, the division contained artillery and support services, so that it could act like a miniature army.

Infantry (3 brigades, each 3-4,000 men strong)

Machine guns (8 per brigade)

Ammunition column

Royal Engineers (two companies)

Howitzer brigade (18 4.5-in howitzers)

Field artillery (3 brigades, each with 18 18-pdr guns)

Heavy artillery (4 60-pdr guns)

Cavalry squadron

Supply train (four companies)

Signals company

Medical section

EUROPE'S ARMIES

FRANCE

During the month of August 1914, France mobilised two million men. The French army was determined to attack the Germans at every opportunity, regardless of casualties.

GERMANY

German forces were the best organised in Europe and had the advantage of a highly trained and efficient general staff – high-ranking officers who directed the movements of troops to and on the battlefield.

BELGIUM

The Belgian army was one of the smallest in Europe, with just 117,000 men. Invaded by Germany in 1914, the Belgians were unable to stop the Germans conquering most of their country, although their army continued to fight with the Allies until 1918.

🙁 OVER BY CHRISTMAS?

Few people had any idea what war would be like. Most soldiers thought it would consist of a few enormous battles which would decide victory, leading to the expression 'the war will be over by Christmas!' They were to be proved very wrong.

Carl von Clemm, a German recruit, explains his emotions on hearing of the outbreak of war:

'It is normal all over the world with young fellows who see war as an adventure. We believed God was on our side. We felt we were defending ourselves, and I was very anxious to be a patriot and help defend my country.'

German troops wave from a railway wagon as they leave for the front in 1914.

🙁 STEAMING TO THE FRONT

The generals on all sides believed that it was essential that their troops be transported to the battlefield as swiftly as possible. In order to invade France and Belgium, the Germans built 13 separate railway lines to carry their troops to the border. The French used 7,000 trains to transport their forces to the front line during August 1914.

The Western Front

In 1914 Germany sent more than 1.5 million troops to fight the French and British in the west, leaving the remainder of their army to tackle Russia in the east.

The German plan required nearly one million men to march through Belgium and northern France, surround the main French force and capture Paris. The plan nearly succeeded, but the French were able to stop the German advance at the Battle of the Marne in September 1914.

By the end of the year, fighting battles on open ground had ended, to be replaced by battles fought from dug-in trenches.

PROFESSIONAL SOLDIERS

Unlike the huge European armies which were made up of conscripts, the British army was a small force made up of large numbers of volunteers.

The British were only able to send 150,000 men to France in August 1914, but they played a major role in blunting the German attack. The British realised they would need many more soldiers and launched a major recruitment drive.

UNIFORMS

Infantry are the foot soldiers of any army. British infantry wore khaki uniforms which helped camouflage (conceal) them from the enemy. In 1914, the French still wore blue coats and bright red trousers, which made them easy targets. In 1915 they adopted a blue-grey uniform.

Infantry cap

BRITISH SOLDIER, 1914

Tunic

Ammunition pouch

Lee Enfield .303 calibre rifle

Haversack

Entrenching tool for digging

'Puttees' (leg wraps)

Leather boots

EQUIPMENT

British steel helmet

German 'pickelhaube' helmet

A SOLDIER'S KIT

As every soldier was expected to fight for several days without receiving extra supplies, he had to carry a lot of equipment with him, including a greatcoat or blanket, food and water and lots of ammunition for his rifle.

Entrenching tool

Bayonet

Ammunition

German Mauser rifle

HELMETS

Shell splinters caused many head wounds. As a result, protective steel helmets were introduced in 1915-16. The British steel helmet came into service in 1916, while the German spiked 'pickelhaube' helmet – made of leather – was replaced by the 'coal-scuttle' steel helmet.

GERMAN INFANTRY KIT

Shoulder straps

Greatcoat

Blanket

Back pack

Bayonet

Food bag

Water bottle

Entrenching tool

WEAPONS AND TOOLS

The main weapon of all infantry was a bolt-action rifle, which had a magazine containing five or 10 cartridges. A well-trained soldier could fire up to 15 shots per minute.

For stabbing at the enemy in close combat, soldiers fixed bayonets to the end of their rifles.

DEFENSIVE FIREPOWER

Artillery, rifles and machine guns proved so effective that soldiers were fatally exposed above ground. As a result, they were forced to dig trenches to survive.

For most of the war troops defending their trenches could always defeat those attacking them across open ground.

FIELD ARTILLERY

The most dangerous weapon on the 1914 battlefield was field artillery, guns light enough to be moved easily and capable of a very high rate of fire.

The best field gun of the war was the French 75mm gun. This fired up to 20 rounds per minute – or one shell every three seconds.

FRENCH 75mm GUN AND CREW

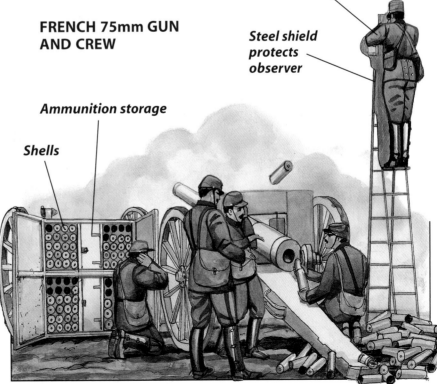

Fire-control observer

Steel shield protects observer

Ammunition storage

Shells

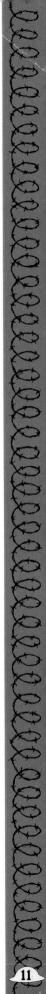

Trench warfare

By 1915 a network of trenches stretched from the Belgian coast to Switzerland. Most trench systems – like the one shown in the main picture – consisted of a front-line trench protected by rolls of barbed wire. Behind this was a support trench and then reserve trenches. They were connected to each other by communication trenches.

In an offensive, soldiers moved up to the front-line trenches. After an artillery bombardment they went 'over the top' (climbed out of their trenches) to attack the enemy. Casualties were generally very heavy because of the greater firepower of the defenders. Men often became entangled in barbed wire and were slaughtered by enemy machine-gun fire.

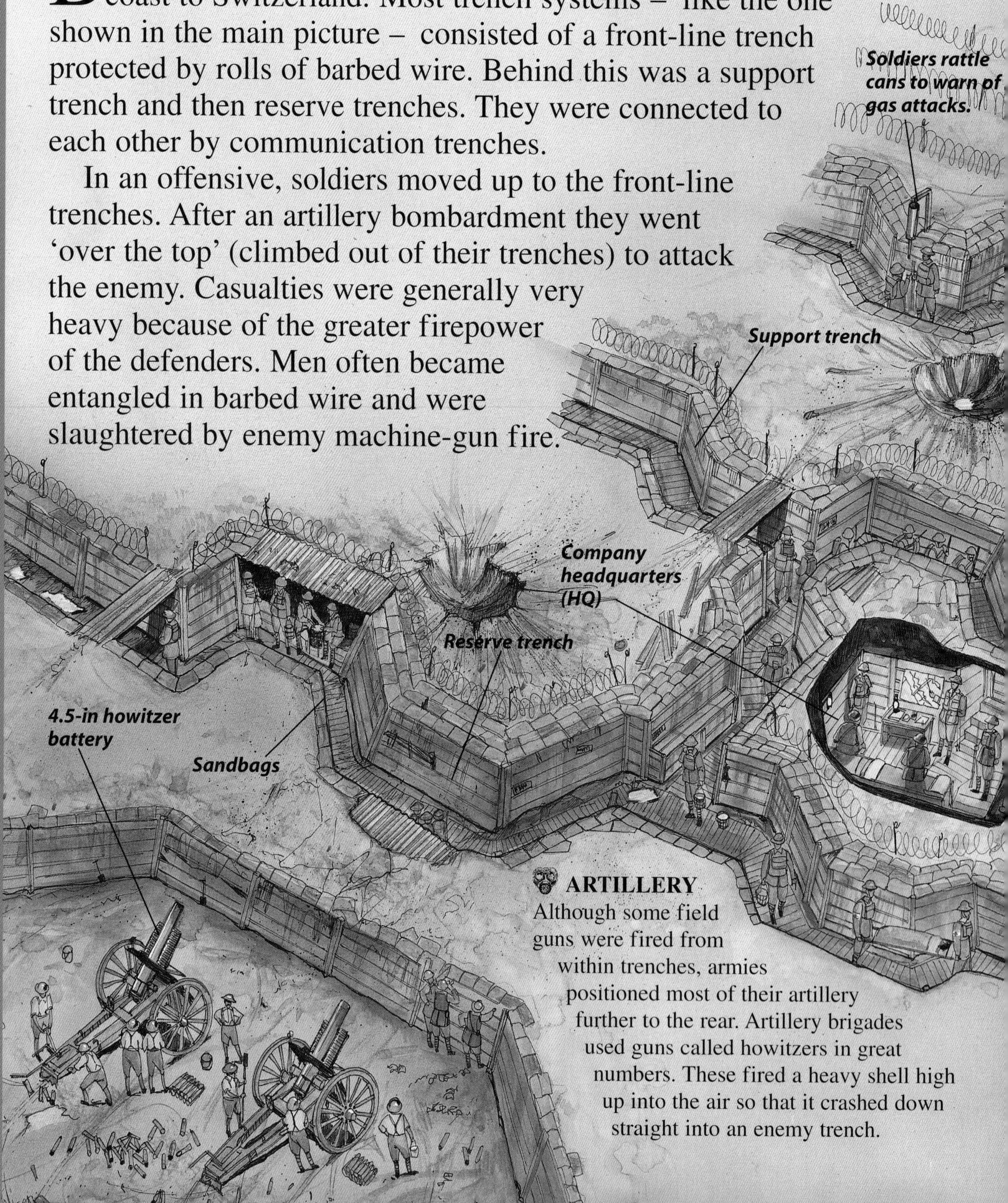

Soldiers rattle cans to warn of gas attacks.

Support trench

Company headquarters (HQ)

Reserve trench

4.5-in howitzer battery

Sandbags

ARTILLERY

Although some field guns were fired from within trenches, armies positioned most of their artillery further to the rear. Artillery brigades used guns called howitzers in great numbers. These fired a heavy shell high up into the air so that it crashed down straight into an enemy trench.

☠ NO MAN'S LAND

Soldiers from each side faced each other across a strip of ground called 'no man's land', which in some places might be as wide as a kilometre but in others might be only 50 metres across. At night, patrols would be sent out to attack the enemy's defences; it was dangerous work.

German trenches

No man's land

Barbed wire

Trench periscope

Front-line trench

Forward observation post

Trench scaling ladders

Light machine gun team

Fire step

Communication trench

TRENCH EQUIPMENT

MACHINE GUNS

Machine guns – such as the British Vickers or the German Maxim – were one of the most deadly weapons on the Western Front. Operated by a two-man crew, the guns fired 400-500 bullets every minute.

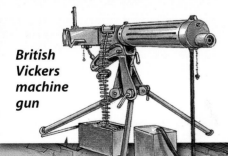

British Vickers machine gun

GAS MASKS

Germany first used poison gas in 1915. Released from cylinders or fired from shells, gas killed men without protective masks. Gas masks were always very uncomfortable to wear.

PERISCOPES

Because it was dangerous to stick your head above the parapet of the trench, troops in the front line used periscopes to peer at the enemy in the trenches opposite.

The mirror at the top of the periscope reflected the view to the observer below.

The experience of war

Life in the trenches was usually grim. Apart from the dangers of enemy artillery and machine-gun fire, soldiers endured plagues of rats and lice. In wet weather the trenches soon became flooded.

Major offensives were quite rare, so that for most of the time soldiers waited, sending out patrols into no man's land, repairing damage and watching for enemy activity. Soldiers worked mainly at night, as it was normally too dangerous for them to move about in daylight.

GENERALSHIP

The generals who commanded the armies of World War One have often been criticised because some people feel they did not care enough about their troops. Over the four years of war, millions of men were killed and wounded on the Western Front, yet very little ground was won by either side.

But World War One was a war where the side that could last longest won the war. In the end, the Allies were just too strong for the Central Powers.

French soldiers hang up their catch of rats.

TRENCH LIFE

Soldiers in the trenches often complained that boredom was their worst enemy. Attempts were made to make life a little more fun, and rat-catching competitions were popular with troops on all sides. Front-line soldiers developed their own special sense of humour, which helped them put up with hardships. Hygiene was also a constant problem in the trenches. It was very difficult to keep clean, and most men became infected with lice, which lived among their clothes and caused diseases. Men spent hours trying to get rid of lice – whose bites were extremely irritating – but they always seemed to return.

Six German soldiers carry a wounded comrade.

💀 MISERY IN THE MUD

Rain turned the battlefield into mud, which was made worse as the ground was churned up by artillery. Trenches collapsed; shell craters became vast pools of slime in which a man could drown in seconds. Moving supplies and guns became virtually impossible, and it could take six to eight men to carry a stretcher (above) which would normally be borne by two soldiers.

This account was written during the Battle of Passchendaele in 1917:

'We heard screaming coming from a crater and there was a fellow up to his shoulders in mud. I said, "Get your rifles and let him get hold of them". But it was no use. The more we pulled and the more he struggled, the further he seemed to go down. And he died. There must have been thousands who died in the mud.'

💀 TRENCH RAIDS

As well as sending out patrols to repair defences and scout for enemy activity, both sides carried out raids. These involved soldiers dashing across no man's land to destroy a section of enemy trench. Silence and surprise were vital.

A typical trench scene – muddy soldiers sheltering behind sandbags and barbed wire.

Behind the lines

Although soldiers spent most of their time in the trenches or working just behind the front line, they were allowed short periods of rest. Once they were away from the trenches, the men could wash – often for the first time in weeks – and have their uniforms cleaned. They would also be able to eat hot, properly cooked food, and have time to get some uninterrupted sleep.

Army commanders realised that time at rest helped their troops recover from the ordeal of being in the front line, so that they would be fitter the next time they were sent into the trenches. Soldiers were encouraged to take part in sports and entertainments.

CANTEENS
The canteen was a shop and a cafe where troops could buy things from home – such as cigarettes, matches and soft drinks – at reasonable prices.

WORK AND PLAY

MAINTENANCE
In the front line, weapons and other pieces of equipment could not be looked after properly. Time behind the lines gave soldiers a chance to mend and maintain equipment, ready for action again in the trenches.

MARKETS
Soldiers were usually paid when they came out of the line, and they were keen to spend it on food and drink. They often bought local produce from Belgian or French civilians. This soldier is buying mistletoe for Christmas celebrations.

SPORT
To keep men fit and healthy, the army encouraged troops to take part in sports, and competitions between units were promoted. Among the more popular sports were football, athletics and boxing and, in cavalry regiments, horse racing.

MEDICAL SERVICES

In World War One medical services were much better than in previous conflicts. Many more wounded men were saved from dying, so that large numbers of them needed long-term care.

A huge network of hospitals was set up behind the Western Front, and tens of thousands of nurses were recruited to look after the wounded. Soldiers who had severe injuries had to be helped to come to terms with their wounds.

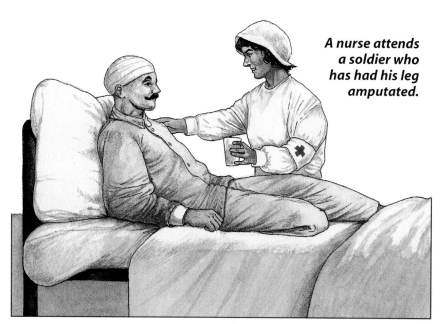

A nurse attends a soldier who has had his leg amputated.

ON WITH THE SHOW

Entertainments were popular and provided an opportunity for men to forget about the trenches – if only for a short while.

Stars were sometimes hired, but usually a unit would provide its own amusement. Soldiers dressed up in the style of entertainers of the day (left) and poked fun at their officers.

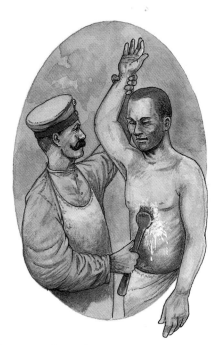

KEEPING CLEAN

After leaving the front line, soldiers marched to huge bathhouses to get rid of the dirt and smell of the trenches. They left their clothes to be cleaned before washing themselves in large tubs holding up to 50 men. When they had finished washing they collected their newly cleaned uniforms. The men were checked to ensure that all lice had been killed, as lice could carry dangerous diseases such as cholera.

An attendant delouses a soldier.

The widening war

In 1915 the Allies declared war on Turkey, whose navy had attacked Russian ports. However, Allied leaders underestimated the fighting ability of Turkish troops and during 1915-16 the Allies were defeated at Gallipoli, and in Palestine (modern Israel and Lebanon) and Mesopotamia (modern Iraq).

Towards the end of 1917 British forces were reorganised and reinforced, and during the following year they repeatedly defeated the Turkish army. In October 1918 the Turks asked the Allies for peace terms.

Leonard Hart, a New Zealand soldier, provided this account of an attack by British soldiers (Tommies) at Gallipoli:

'We could clearly see the Tommies charging across the flat [ground], under a perfect mass of bursting shells and shrapnel. The scrub with which the flat was covered caught fire, and I afterwards heard that many of the wounded, unable to escape, were burnt to death in it.'

Australian and New Zealand troops land at Anzac Cove, near Gallipoli, in 1915.

BEACH LANDINGS

In 1915 Allied troops landed at beaches around Gallipoli. They hoped to defeat the Turks and then march on the Turkish capital of Constantinople (modern Istanbul). But the landings were a disaster – Allied troops were poorly led and unable to push the Turks back from their defensive positions. During the Gallipoli campaign, Australian and New Zealand troops also fought with great courage.

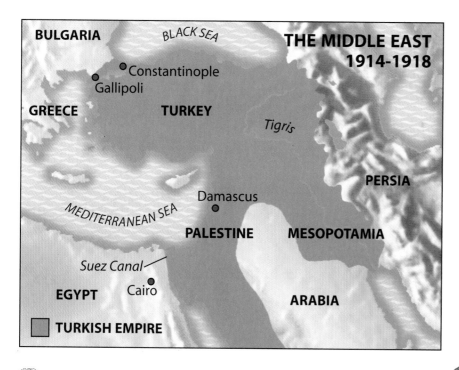

THE MIDDLE EAST 1914-1918

BULGARIA
BLACK SEA
Constantinople
Gallipoli
GREECE
TURKEY
Tigris
PERSIA
MEDITERRANEAN SEA
Damascus
PALESTINE
MESOPOTAMIA
Suez Canal
EGYPT
Cairo
ARABIA
☐ TURKISH EMPIRE

TURKISH TROOPS

Turkish infantry soldiers were highly respected by their Allied opponents because of their toughness. German officers helped train and equip the Turkish army, and a German general, Liman von Sanders, played an important part in defeating the Allies at Gallipoli. The Turks fought with great determination until their final defeat in 1918.

A Turkish infantryman

THE TURKISH EMPIRE

In 1914 the Turkish empire not only included modern Turkey but large areas of the Middle East. The British were afraid the Turks might invade Egypt and capture the Suez Canal – Britain's vital link with her possessions in the East.

To prevent this, the British invaded Palestine and, after many setbacks, captured the key city of Damascus in 1918. In Mesopotamia, the British eventually forced the Turks to retreat back along the River Tigris. After the war, Turkey lost its empire.

T E Lawrence on a camel

LAWRENCE OF ARABIA

A British officer, Colonel T E Lawrence, was sent on a mission to help the Arab peoples fight the Turks, who then ruled over much of Arabia. Lawrence led the Arabs in a guerrilla war against the Turks in the desert.

Using camels and horses, the Arabs destroyed the main Turkish railway system in Arabia and captured the key port of Aqaba. Lawrence's exploits made him a legend.

Conflict in the east

Although the Russians suffered heavy defeats fighting the Germans in 1914, they helped the western Allies (France and Britain) by drawing away German troops from the war on the Western Front. Russia scored more successes against the army of the Austro-Hungarian empire, which had to be reinforced with German troops in order to survive.

During 1915 the Germans began to force the Russians back into their own country, and by 1917 the Russian army was at the point of collapse. In 1917 a revolution in Russia overthrew the Tsar (emperor), and the new Bolshevik, or communist, government asked the Germans for a peace treaty. As a result, parts of Russia came under German control.

Soldier of the Czech Legion

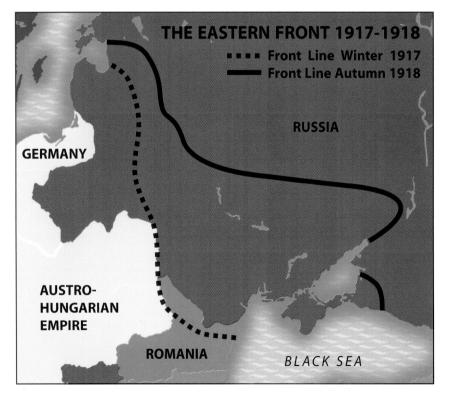

THE EASTERN FRONT 1917-1918

▪▪▪▪ **Front Line Winter 1917**
━━━ **Front Line Autumn 1918**

GERMANY

RUSSIA

AUSTRO-HUNGARIAN EMPIRE

ROMANIA

BLACK SEA

💀 AGAINST THE WAR

The Austro-Hungarian empire was made up of many nations, some of them opposed to the war. One of these was Czechoslovakia, and although Czechs were forced into the army they were reluctant to fight the Russians. Czechs wanted independence, and the Czech Legion was set up to fight for an independent state.

💀 WARFARE ON THE EASTERN FRONT

On the Western Front fighting became bogged down in mud, but in the east, warfare was more open, and armies marched long distances to fight.

The German army did most of the fighting against the Russians, and defeated them on a number of occasions.

THE RUSSIAN ARMY

Ordinary Russian soldiers fought with great bravery, often in terrible conditions, but they were poorly led and often lacked the right weapons and equipment to take on the German army. Among the most elite Russian units was the Cossack cavalry.

During 1916 Allied weapons and equipment began to reach the Russian army, but this was too late to prevent the army's collapse in the following year.

Elite Russian Cossack cavalry trooper

THE TSAR

Tsar Nicholas II was ruler of Russia, and in 1915 he took over direct command of the army. He proved to be a poor commander-in-chief, however, and he eventually lost the respect of the army – and his own people.

After his overthrow in the revolution he was imprisoned by the Bolsheviks, and killed by them in 1918.

The Tsar reviews his army (left).

THE REVOLUTION

In the spring of 1917 the Russian people were short of food and fed up with the war. They rose up against the Tsar and his government. A new government was set up in March, but in November 1917 the Bolsheviks seized power and asked for peace with the Germans.

LENIN

Vladimir Ilyich Lenin was the chief Bolshevik leader. He promised Russians an end to the war and the right to run their own affairs. This made the Bolsheviks popular, especially among soldiers, and their support helped the Bolsheviks to gain power. Once in power, the Bolsheviks set up a dictatorial state.

Bolshevik leader V I Lenin

The war at sea

Britain and Germany were the two main naval rivals. The British had a bigger fleet and imposed a naval blockade on Germany. This prevented ships from leaving or entering German ports. Apart from one attempt to break the blockade at the Battle of Jutland, the main German fleet stayed in port throughout the war.

Instead of taking on the British navy directly, the Germans attacked British merchant ships with U-boats (submarines). This strategy was very effective, and by early 1917 Britain was on the verge of starvation.

WARSHIPS

The modern battleship was the most important fighting ship of World War One. The first of these vessels was HMS *Dreadnought*, launched in 1906. This type of battleship was equipped with heavy guns in armoured turrets; the most modern ships had 15-in guns which could fire a shell up to 18 kilometres.

Dreadnoughts were protected by heavy steel armour which made them hard to sink, while their powerful turbine engines gave them a fast top speed of up to 25 knots (45 km/h).

HMS **Royal Oak** *fires its huge guns, which were housed in swivelling armoured turrets.*

BATTLE OF JUTLAND

The Battle of Jutland was the one great naval engagement of the war. It was fought in the North Sea between 31 May and 1 June 1916. The Germans commanded by Admiral Scheer had hoped to trap part of the British fleet, but during the course of the battle the Germans were themselves nearly caught by the more powerful British force. Realising their danger, the Germans skilfully withdrew.

SEA WARFARE

DESTROYERS
The destroyer was a light and fast warship capable of speeds up to 30 knots (55 km/h). A destroyer's main task was to attack larger ships with its torpedoes, although it also used depth charges against submarines.

SUBMARINES
Armed with a gun and torpedoes, German U-boats sank more than 2,500 Allied vessels. The U-boats were eventually defeated by the Allies who used anti-submarine warfare weapons such as depth charges, and shepherded merchant ships into convoys (fleets) guarded by destroyers.

GERMAN COMMANDER
Admiral Reinhard Scheer became commander of the German High Seas Fleet in 1916, and led his forces into battle at Jutland. Although forced to retreat to port, Scheer claimed victory because the Germans had sunk a few more ships than the British.

THE *LUSITANIA*
The *Lusitania* was a British transatlantic liner, which was sunk by a German U-boat off Ireland on 7 May 1915. Among the 1,198 passengers and crew who drowned were 128 American citizens.

At the time, the United States was a neutral country, but the sinking of the *Lusitania* caused outrage in America and turned public opinion against Germany.

A contemporary picture of the Lusitania incident conveys the horror of the sinking.

AMERICA ENTERS THE WAR
Germany's determination to starve Britain into submission using submarines also meant that many American ships trading with Britain were sunk. German leaders knew that they were angering the United States but they thought it was a risk worth taking. They were wrong. The USA declared war on Germany on 6 April 1917, and a powerful army was sent to France to help fight the Germans.

New methods of warfare

By the end of 1916, the armies of both sides on the Western Front were beginning to learn some of the lessons of trench warfare. They used new weapons and tactics to help troops cross no man's land. Among the weapons were new types of poison gas, light machine guns, mortars and tanks. Soldiers were better trained: they fought in small groups that supported each other.

The most important change, however, came in new ways of using artillery. Gunners perfected the 'creeping barrage' so that as the infantry advanced, the artillery's fire 'advanced' just ahead of them. Guns became more accurate, and fired special shells such as smoke shells to hide an infantry advance.

COMMUNICATIONS
The main way for a commander to keep in touch with his troops was by field telephone, but the wires were often cut in an attack. As a result, soldiers and animals – such as homing pigeons and dogs – passed on messages.

TANKS

ARMOURED MONSTER
The German army was not very impressed by tanks, and only built 16 A7Vs. This mobile fortress had a crew of up to 18 men and five machine guns. It was too clumsy to be effective.

LIGHT AND POPULAR
The Renault FT-17 light tank had a two-man crew and was armed with a machine gun or cannon. The FT-17 supported infantry attacks during the battles of 1918. It was popular with American troops.

FAMOUS FIRST
The British army used tanks for the first time during the Battle of the Somme in September 1916, but they were very unreliable and had a top road speed of just 5 km/h. By 1918 tanks became more reliable – and more useful.

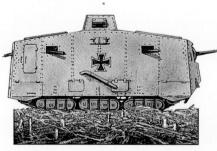

A British tank attacks German front-line troops.

🪖 BATTLE OF CAMBRAI

The Battle of Cambrai, which began on 20 November 1917, was the first time that tanks led a major offensive (above).

The Germans were taken completely by surprise and were driven from their trenches, but within a couple of days most of the tanks had broken down or been destroyed by German artillery. The attack ground to a halt as the Germans rushed up reinforcements.

🪖 WAR UNDERGROUND

On the Western Front mines were used by both sides. Troops dug long tunnels underneath the enemy trenches and packed them full of high explosives (below).

When the explosives were set off, they could totally destroy the enemy's front-line trench. If the enemy discovered a mine, they might dig a countermine in order to cut off and destroy the original mine.

🪖 ARTIFICIAL TREES

To provide good observation positions, soldiers made artificial tree stumps from steel cylinders covered with wire mesh and canvas (above). Troops put these up at night next to an existing tree stump, which would then be removed so that the enemy would think that the false tree was real.

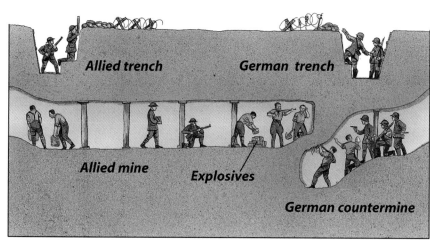

Allied trench   German trench

Allied mine   Explosives

German countermine

Battle in the skies

The greatest advance in technology during the war came not on land or at sea but in the air. Within the space of four years, the rickety aeroplanes of 1914 had become effective war machines.

The size of air forces also grew enormously: in 1914 Britain went to war with around 100 unarmed aircraft; by 1918 the newly formed Royal Air Force (RAF) had 22,000 aircraft of all types. Aviation was seen as a new and glamorous activity; pilots came to be regarded as heroes.

A British Sopwith Camel chases a German Fokker triplane during an aerial dogfight.

THE ARMY'S EYES

The main function of the air force in World War One was reconnaissance – to see what the enemy was doing in and behind their front line.

From 1917, aircraft began to be fitted with simple radio sets so that observers could tell gunners where their shells were landing.

DOGFIGHTS

At first, aircraft were unarmed but soon pilots began to carry pistols and rifles to shoot at each other. By 1915 machine guns were in use. The new fighter aircraft protected their own reconnaissance aircraft as well as shooting down enemy planes. By 1916, huge aerial battles or 'dogfights' were common. Pilots who had shot down five or more aircraft were known as 'aces'. These included German Manfred von Richthofen (80 kills), Frenchman René Fonck (75 kills) and British pilot Edward 'Mick' Mannock (73 kills).

AIRCRAFT

FAST AND EFFECTIVE
The SE5a was one of the best British fighters of the war, capable of taking on any German aircraft. The SE5a was armed with two machine guns and had a top speed of 202 km/h.

POPULAR CHOICE
The French SPAD fighter was highly popular among French and American pilots. The SPAD XIII was armed with two machine guns and had a top speed of more than 210 km/h.

DEADLY RAIDER
Gotha bombers were used in raids on London and Paris. They carried up to 500 kg of bombs, although their slow maximum speed of 142 km/h made them vulnerable targets for Allied fighter aircraft.

🐞 AIRSHIPS
Both the Allies and the Germans used airships during the war. Most German models were built by Count Zeppelin.

These 'Zeppelins' used hydrogen gas to keep them in the air, and although not very fast they could travel long distances – at least 2,000 kilometres. They were mainly used for reconnaissance and to bomb cities in Britain and France. Zeppelins flew higher than most aircraft, and so were safe from attack. But by 1917 improved fighter aeroplanes could fly higher and were thus able to shoot the Zeppelins down.

🐞 ALL-AMERICAN ACE
American Eddie Rickenbacker (above) was a motor racing driver before the war, and it was only in March 1918 that he became a pilot. Despite his late start, Rickenbacker was a natural fighter pilot and soon began to build up a good score of kills.

When the war ended he had shot down at least 26 enemy aircraft, making him the highest-scoring American pilot.

German Zeppelin L-50

The last year of the war

By early 1918 the Allied blockade of German ports was causing great hardship, and people were beginning to starve. The arrival of American troops in France also meant that Allied troops greatly outnumbered the Germans. The German commanders then tried a desperate gamble to win the war.

The end of the war on the Eastern Front had freed German troops, and they were sent to the West to spearhead a last great offensive. Although the Germans did well at first, the Allied line held.

During the summer of 1918 the Allies themselves went on the offensive and forced the German armies back. Realising that the war was lost, the Germans agreed to armistice talks on 11 November 1918.

An American infantryman, known as a 'doughboy'

🎭 THE US ARRIVES

When the United States declared war in April 1917, its army was small and not yet trained for modern warfare.

After America entered the war the US army expanded rapidly, so that by November 1918 there were more than two million trained American soldiers in France.

🎭 GERMAN PRISONERS

During the great Allied offensive of 1918, German troops began to surrender in large numbers for the first time. The Allied forces were just too strong and the ordinary German soldier was becoming sick of the war. On a single day – 29 September – British troops captured more than 35,000 Germans.

A British soldier takes a German prisoner.

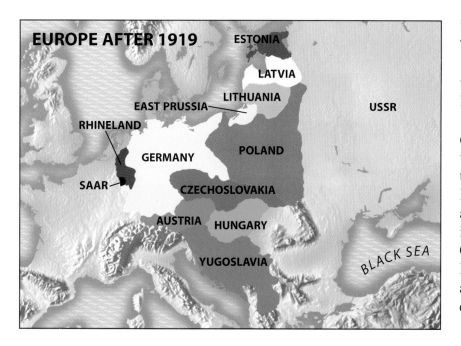

EUROPE AFTER 1919

ESTONIA
LATVIA
LITHUANIA
EAST PRUSSIA
USSR
RHINELAND
GERMANY
POLAND
SAAR
CZECHOSLOVAKIA
AUSTRIA
HUNGARY
YUGOSLAVIA
BLACK SEA

TREATY OF VERSAILLES

The treaty signed at Versailles in 1919 reorganised Europe, and as the losers of the war the Central Powers suffered most.

Germany lost lands in the east to the state of Poland and was made to give up some of its territory to France. The Austro-Hungarian empire was broken up and new states put in its place, including the newly independent Czechoslovakia. In addition, the Baltic states of Lithuania, Latvia and Estonia were created at the expense of Russia.

VICTORY CELEBRATIONS

In the Allied nations, the end of the war was greeted with wild enthusiasm, and people flocked into the streets to celebrate. But in four years of fighting over 13 million soldiers had been killed, and Europe had lost much of its wealth paying for the war.

Only the United States profited from the conflict – after 1918 it was confirmed as the world's most powerful industrial nation.

A French soldier returns home.

AN END TO THE FIGHTING

Once the Central Powers had accepted defeat, the great armies began to demobilise.

Those soldiers who had survived the war were now able to go home, but the process was slow – many men had to remain in the army until the end of 1919, which caused great bitterness.

When news of the end of the war reached London, people crowded onto the streets to celebrate:

'There was great liveliness, calls, cries, whistles and hooters sounding, noise and crowds. Great happiness prevailed. Every vehicle … was boarded by people, most of whom waved flags.'

Glossary

Allies
The name given to the states of France, Russia, Britain and Belgium, who waged war against the Central Powers. The Allies were later joined by Italy, Greece, Japan and the United States.

Blockade
The policy adopted by the Allies to prevent ships carrying food and other goods from entering German ports.

Bolshevik
A member of the extreme left-wing political party led by the Russian revolutionary V I Lenin. It later became the Communist Party.

Central Powers
The states of Germany, Austria-Hungary, Turkey and Bulgaria, who waged war against the Allies.

Conscription
A military system adopted by most countries in Europe in which young men were required to serve in the army or navy for approximately two years before returning to civilian life.

In the event of war, the country could quickly call large numbers of men with military training back into the armed forces.

Demobilise
The process of reducing the size of a nation's armed forces by allowing servicemen to return to civilian life. The opposite of mobilisation.

Dictatorial state
A type of government in which the people have little or no say in how the country is run. The Bolsheviks replaced the dictatorial state of the Tsar with one of their own.

Dogfight
A battle fought in the air between two groups of opposing fighter aircraft.

Field gun
A light artillery piece that fired shrapnel and high explosive directly at enemy troops.

Guerrilla war
A type of war in which a small guerrilla force does not take on a large enemy army in a conventional battle, but uses surprise and deception to conduct raids against outposts and minor strong points.

T E Lawrence helped lead an Arab force in a guerrilla war against the Turkish army in Arabia.

British Vickers machine gun

Howitzer

An artillery piece that lobs a shell containing explosives high into the air so that it comes down on the enemy almost vertically. Howitzers were very effective in smashing trenches and dugouts.

Light machine gun

Although very effective, standard machine guns were too heavy to carry around on the battlefield, so the light machine gun was developed. It could be carried by a two-man crew. The British Lewis gun was an early example of a light machine gun.

Infantryman of the Czech Legion

Merchant shipping

Civilian ships that carried cargoes of food and other goods from one country to another. Unlike naval ships, they did not usually carry any weapons, and they were very vulnerable to attacks by U-boats (submarines).

Mobilisation

The act of making a country's armed forces ready for war. Civilians who had already trained as conscripts would be immediately called up to serve in the armed forces.

Mortar

A simple and lightweight piece of artillery used by the infantry. Similar to a miniature howitzer, a mortar lobbed a small shell up to a great height.

No man's land

The strip of ground that separated the two opposing trench systems.

Reconnaissance

The way in which an army finds out about the position and movement of enemy forces. Aircraft play a major role in providing reconnaissance for the armies of both sides.

Lookout post

Revolution

The violent overthrow of a government or political system. The Russian revolution of 1917 was one of the key events during World War One.

Torpedo

A long underwater missile that was fired from submarines and destroyers to sink enemy ships.

Western Front

The battleground in France and Belgium where Germany fought the Allies. It consisted of a line of trenches stretching from the Belgian coast to Switzerland.

INDEX

PHOTOGRAPHIC CREDITS:
Mary Evans Picture Library
  p. 23
Hulton Getty Collection
  pp. 15, 18, 21, 29
Robert Hunt Picture Library
  pp. 9, 17

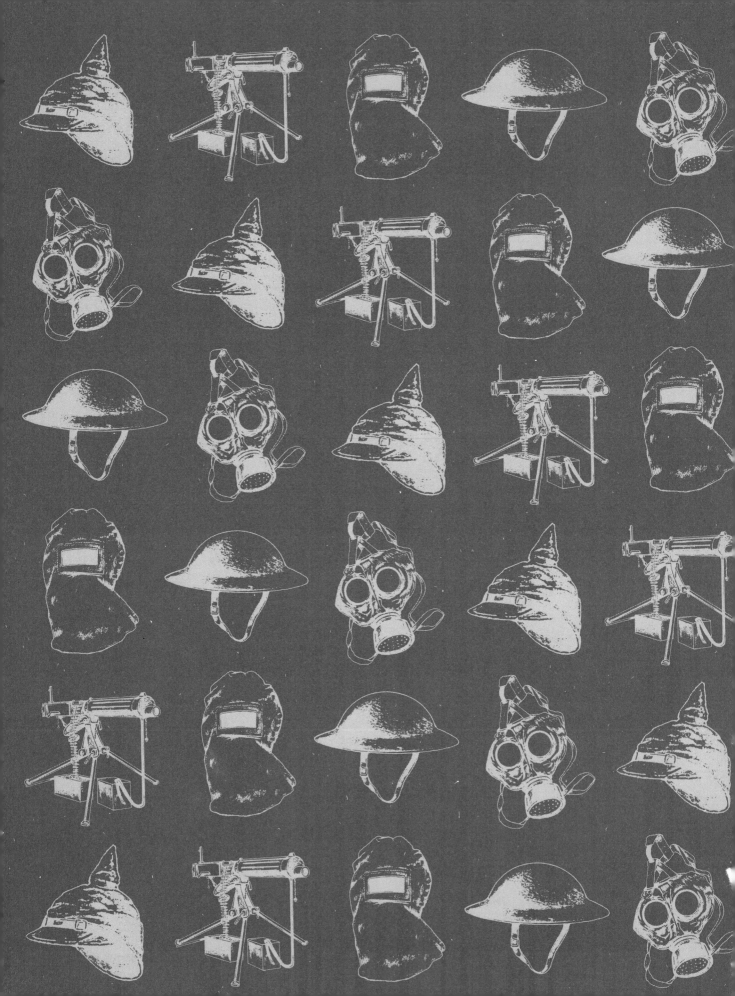